Never Surrender: How to Overcome Life's Greatest Challenges

By

Joseph B. George

Copyright 2017 by Joseph B. George

All rights reserved.

No part of this book may be reproduced, stored in a retrieval system, or transmitted by any means, electronic, mechanical, photocopying, recording, or otherwise, without written permission from the author.

Acknowledgements

Thank you for your love, support, wisdom, and knowledge! The late Reverend Joseph C. George, Mary George, Jennifer George, Melanie Little, Jodi George, Joseph G. George, Marilyn Henry, Dr. Sydney Barnwell, Dr. Sarah V. Kirk, Dr. Jay Snell

Table of Contents

Introduction 1
Chapter 1: Training 2
Chapter 2: Preparing for Deployment 6
Chapter 3: Saudi Arabia 10
Chapter 4: Air War 14
Chapter 5: The Attack 17
Chapter 6: Impact of War 25
Chapter 7: Rehabilitation 33
Chapter 8: Life After Rehabilitation 39
Chapter 9: Problems Aren't Coincidental 43
Chapter10: How to Overcome 45
Recommended Reading 55
About the Author 56
Contact Joseph 57

Introduction

In 1991, I was an M1 Tanker in the 1st Infantry Division, U.S. Army. (Big Red One) It's America's most lethal division, and tanks lead the way. The life expectancy for a tanker was about 15 minutes in battle.

Our mission was to lead the attack on the enemy mine field while being attacked by chemical and biological weapons. It was a suicide mission, and we were awarded the Valorous Unit Award for extraordinary heroism in war. Tankers don't surrender! We had months to think about the suicide mission and death before the Gulf War started.

I survived the war, but the impact that it had on my life was devastating. Doctors don't know where the illnesses come from, and there is no cure for many of the diseases. Twenty-two veterans commit suicide daily because of stress.

The information in this book isn't ordinary. This book will show you why your problems aren't a coincidence and how to overcome your greatest challenges!

Chapter 1

Training

Combat is a life-changing event that affects the human spirit tremendously. Soldiers enter combat not knowing that their lives will be changed forever. Before the first bullet is ever fired, the soldier's mind is numb, and he is prepared to give his life for his country.

After I had graduated from high school, I did my basic training at Ft. Knox, Kentucky which is the home of Armor. That is where I was introduced to modern warfare. I certainly did not know what I was in for, but I was young and extremely cocky. The first thing I learned was not to even think about disobeying orders. I was pushed mentally and physically further than I could ever imagine. High school football was a joke compared to basic training.

The culture shock began when I stepped off the bus at Ft. Knox, Kentucky. We ran off the bus to screaming drill sergeants, ordering us to form lines. Drill sergeant Conyers was over 6 feet tall and all muscle. I tried to run away from him, but he called me back to his platoon. They told us that we would never forget our drill sergeants and they were right. It was drill sergeants Kay and Conyers' job to transform us into soldiers, and they did a tremendous job.

We were different from anyone else at Ft. Knox because we were tankers, the backbone of the U.S. Army. We trained harder and longer than everyone else. The tank is the most superior and feared weapon on the battlefield when it comes to ground warfare. The first time I saw a M1A1 Abrams tank I was overwhelmed. It was 60 tons of steel and had a top speed of 50 mph. I was 18 when I graduated from basic training, and I was in the best shape of my life.

Furthermore, I was stationed at Ft. Riley, Kansas, with the 1st Infantry Division, also known as the Big Red One. My first day at work my unit was in the field, and they placed me on the commander's tank. That is where I learned that the average tank battle lasts about 15 minutes. I also learned how to fight the Soviet Union. This training would prove to be vital during Desert Storm.

The first time I pulled battalion duty, I realized how much tradition the Big Red One has. I slept in a room with spectacular pictures of the division in Vietnam. It was simply amazing. They were valiant soldiers and had hearts like gladiators. It put me in the frame of mind to fight to the death with everything I had. I was making the transition to becoming a killing machine. I was starting to understand where the nickname "No Mission too Difficult, No Sacrifice too Great, Duty First!" came from. However, it was 1990, and I didn't think a war would break out in 2 years. Little did I know that I was about to be placed on the front lines of the battlefield with the most destructive fire power the world had ever seen.

M-1 Tankers spend an enormous amount of time in the field training for battle. It was 65 degrees below zero with the wind chill factor, and we had to train as if it were 70 degrees. If you took your gloves off for longer than 10 seconds, you would be frostbitten, and your flesh could stick to the steel. My tank was my home. All I could do at night under those conditions was tap my feet on the floor to keep my circulation going. I was assigned to Delta Company 2nd Battalion, 34th Armor, and we were Top Guns. Our motto was "Dreadnaught." Every month we would simulate fighting the Soviet Union in the field. Once a year we went to the National Training Center in California to simulate fighting the Soviet Union for 30 days. That is where I learned how deadly combat really was. For example, if my tank was disabled, we would still fight it sitting still. Tankers don't surrender under any circumstances.

Meanwhile, In August 1990, we were at the gunnery range at Fort Riley when we learned that Iraq had invaded Kuwait. Immediately rumors were spreading like wildfire that we were going. Unlike the National Training Center in California, we lived in the barracks for two weeks, and we had access to television. Secretary of State Dick Cheney flew in, escorted by Black Hawk helicopters to check the status of our readiness. While the tanks were firing on the range, he was nervously jumping around, shaking his head "yes." He asked me how old I was and why I joined the Army. I told him I joined to pay for college. He was extremely intelligent.

Furthermore, he took some pictures with my tank crew and left. After we had returned from the gunnery range, we started preparing to deploy to the Gulf, even though we had not received orders. Finally, while watching CNN on our lunch break, we learned that we were deploying.

Chapter 2

Preparing for Deployment

The first objective was to get the tanks painted. It did not take long at all to get this done. However, we did spend long hours in the night doing it, but we knew how important it was that everything was done right. Next was the dangerous job of driving the tanks on the trains. It was done without any injuries or fatalities. It was an awesome sight to see all those heavies lined up waiting for action. It gave us a sense of invincibility. The tanks were railed to a port in Beaumont, Texas. The division's equipment was shipped to Saudi Arabia from there.

I made my will and gave my mother power of attorney. My company commander told us that he was not authorizing us to go home for the holidays, but he was not telling us not to go. We knew not to miss the flight to Saudi Arabia. Meanwhile, my company was going to be the first tanks to clear the Iraqi minefields. Everyone knew that a tank battle lasted about 15 minutes and it was clear that we would not leave the mine fields alive.

At this point, we still did not know the exact date we were leaving, and it was almost Christmas Eve. I was 19, and none of my family members had ever missed a Christmas, and I was not about to start now. I talked to my buddy from Louisiana, and he felt the same way. He said he would never miss a Christmas if he was in the United States. We knew we were not coming home from the war and it was Christmas. Three of us drove to the airport in a blizzard. It was so cold in Kansas that the gas was frozen in the pump.

I went home for Christmas, thinking this could be my last time seeing my family and friends. I had the best friends in the world. My family was great, and it was Christmas. Christmas Day, my mother sent my cousin to find me because I hung out all night. I took some family photos and said my last goodbyes. On the way to the airport, I told my mother to make one last stop at my best friend's house. When I walked in, his family was eating Christmas dinner at the table and tears were rolling down my face. His dad was a Vietnam Veteran with a purple heart, and he immediately stood up. My best friend told me that I was coming back, but he did not know what I knew.

Finally, I was at the airport, and I hugged my family for the last time. I saw a guy in my company at the airport in Charlotte that was not supposed to be there. He had dark sunglasses on, and we hardly said anything to each other because of the situation at hand. He had a look on his face of a man that had seen his family for the last time. It was as if he had the world on his shoulders. He knew it was all over and he was preparing mentally to fight this war. We had too much on our minds to sit together on the plane. The situation was becoming tremendously intense.

Everyone that went home returned safely. During physical training, the captain asked me how my trip was. I told him it was great. He did not ask me if I went home, but it seemed like he knew.

Those are the kind of guys that you want to go to war with. The orders came down that we would leave on New Year's Eve. Some soldiers were breaking down mentally. The pressure of the mission was taking its toll, and we were forced to keep each other together. In war, you are only as good as the guy beside you.

It was like a bad dream. The reality was, we were not coming back. I was only 19, and I was in a no-win situation. We could not drink any alcohol within 48 hours of departing. The barracks were so quiet on New Year's Eve that you could hear a pin drop.

I kept checking my duffle bag repeatedly to make sure I had all of my equipment. I saw a gunner from South Carolina lying on his bed, watching everything that passed by his room. He was terrified.

He could not believe that we were not coming back. Everything that we trained for was about to be tested.

We knew that we had to clear the mine field for the rest of the ground forces to fight at all costs. That was the only job given to us because we would not make it out alive. One thing was for sure: it would be short and devastating. I played the scenarios in my head to prepare myself for destruction and certain death. It did not matter what anyone said or thought. This was the ultimate sacrifice, and it was no joke.

At this point, I had crossed the line of no return. It was all about doing my job the best I could. I had no intentions of losing or surrendering. It was all or nothing. I made up in my mind that I would do everything I possibly could to make it back home alive, but I was at peace with death. On the 21-hour flight to Saudi Arabia, my friend from Louisiana showed me some card tricks. We stopped in Belgium to refuel.

Chapter 3

Saudi Arabia

We arrived in Saudi Arabia on New Year's Day, 1991. We lived in tents until we moved out closer to Iraq. About two weeks later, our ship arrived while we were playing tag football in the desert. The ship was escorted by Apache attack helicopters. It was the first time I had seen an Apache in person, and it was an awesome sight to see.

We stopped playing football to take in the moment. Play time was over, and it was time to get down to business. Our tanks were unloaded and inspected.

We were not supposed to use those tanks because we had new ones waiting for us in Germany, if we ever fought the Soviet Union. We used the new tanks that were more sophisticated and had more firepower. The National Guard received our old tanks.

Some marines came over to look at our tanks, and they were amazed at the firepower. The M1A1 tank has one .50- caliber machine gun, one M-16 rifle, 2 grenade launchers, two 240 machine guns, and one

120mm cannon. My personal weapon was a 9-millimeter pistol.

The Marines knew they did not have anything that could match it, and they were amazed. However, I got a chance to see the Apaches up close. They were awesome. A tank is defenseless against air assaults, and it crossed my mind many times.

Trucks called HETS moved our 60-ton tanks closer to Iraq. Saudi buses transported us to our tanks. Rumors were circulating that the King of Saudi Arabia offered each American soldier $9,000 if the U.S. sent women home and $6,000 if they did not. The U.S. said that we were not mercenaries.

Meanwhile, we stayed at one location and moved out frequently. Life is very uncomfortable, living on a tank. I walked about 50 yards from the tank and dug a hole to defecate.

One day I was standing on top of my tank, and an A-10 Warthog (war plane) was coming directly towards me. I was helpless, and I thought I was going to die. I was so scared that I defecated in my pants. It's big, bulky, and its main job is to destroy tanks. The reason a tank battle is so short is because there is so much firepower on the battlefield, and tanks are the main target.

Most of the time was spent waiting for the war to start in the desert. That was very unusual because we worked most of the time. That gave us more time to think about the situation.

However, we did test our weapons systems in the desert. The 120mm cannon packed a tremendous punch. That's when I found out that the rounds were made from depleted uranium. I also knew that nuclear submarines were ready to launch a nuclear attack if needed. Rumors swirled that if the war got out of hand, the Arab nations would fight with Iraq.

For some reason, I was not worried about a chemical attack, even though the threat was there. I daydreamed most of the time about going to college and raising a family. I was switched to the executive officer's tank with the guy that was in the airport in Charlotte. The gunner was from New York, the driver was from Georgia, the commander was from Ohio, and I was from North Carolina. We got along and worked well together.

However, the pressure was mounting as the deadline to leave Kuwait drew closer. I was 19, and I had never seen a grown man scared. My mind was set on the task at hand. We knew we were going to fight, and Saddam promised a bloody fight. We were up to the challenge.

While sitting around waiting, an armored Iraqi vehicle rolled into our location. Someone quickly destroyed it. Nothing was ever said about the incident because we knew what awaited us.

I saw a tank shoot another tank in the rear before the ground war started. The tank that was hit was getting ready to shoot back, but a ceasefire came over the radio. Again, no questions were asked, because we knew the situation at hand.

The enemy had time to build a trench on the border of Saudi Arabia, and Iraq filled with mines to stop us from entering Iraq. We knew that they would use chemical and biological weapons on us. That is why it was predicted that the first tanks through would not survive. Although we were in a no-win situation, our morale remained high. We were going to fight to the death.

We had plenty of firepower, so we were confident. We also had something to come back for. Even though they said we were not coming back, it would not be because we did not give the effort.

The last stop before combat was the Saudi-Iraqi border. Iraqi soldiers tried to cross the border at night, and we picked them off with machine guns. Our night vision capabilities were amazing.

Chapter 4

Air War

The air war started, and Operation Desert Shield was now Operation Desert Storm. We listened to the news on the British Broadcasting Channel with our Walkman radios. The Allied Forces' air power did a tremendous job.

It was not long before I could see the burning flames over Baghdad. The sky was orange at night because of the bombing raids. We waited anxiously as the B-52 bombers dropped their massive bombs. Sometimes the ground would shake after a B-52 strike.

It was an awesome sight, to see B-52s escorted by fighters. We controlled the sky, and it was a comforting feeling. The air campaign dominated the Iraqi military; no stone was left unturned.

The United States bombed Iraq 24 hours a day, and the results were devastating. During the weeks of the air war, I had time to think about every situation that I was going to face. It was the first time that I was not busy since I joined the Army.

After a month of intense bombing, it was time for the ground war to begin. War cannot be won by airpower alone, and the tank is the king of the battlefield. The captain gave the orders that the ground war would start February 24, 1991.

The original plan had not changed. Our objective was to clear the Iraqi mine field so the rest of the 7th Corp could pass through. We were going through Iraq while everyone else attacked Kuwait.

Everything had come down to this. It was the moment of truth. My entire unit was ready. We were prepared to fight until the bitter end. The word "surrender" was never mentioned. I felt like I had the firepower I needed to get the job done.

When the Big Red One spread out and prepared for battle, I saw tanks for as far as my eyes could see. We had over 360 tanks. I did not realize that we had that much firepower, even though we had 4 battalions of tanks.

I was waiting for the Air force to bomb the mine field, but it never happened. A tank commander who was also an Army Ranger gave a message over the radio that revealed the intensity of the situation. The tone of his voice was incredibly strange. It was as if he were already dead. I don't know why the captain did not give that speech.

The night before we attacked, the refueler told me that I better get as much fuel as possible, because he did not want to be anywhere near a tank when the battle started. He was terrified, and I understood why. There's nowhere to hide in the desert, and tanks are the number one target. We expected them to use chemicals, so we put on our chemical suits.

The captain gave one last briefing that night before we attacked. We hardly talked, because we were focusing on what we had to do. There are a million things that can go wrong in war, and you must be prepared.

Nothing beats preparation. The United States usually strikes at night, because of our night vision advantage. The driver of my tank told me that his last unit's motto is "hell on wheels, we strike at night."

Chapter 5

The Attack

We attacked before dawn. There were two green lights that we were supposed to pass through that no one on my tank saw. Suddenly, my tank crew was lost in total darkness.

We kept asking the commander for help, and all he said was keep going north. I had already seen the friendly fire incident, and I knew that the enemy was north. I did not know if I would be killed by friendly or enemy fire. At the same time, tanks were opening fire on anything that was out there.

I did not want to die like that. My adrenaline was flowing to full capacity. This was not supposed to happen, and we had not planned for it. I had lost it, and I was awaiting death. I felt helpless, and I was a sitting duck.

When dawn came, my tank was cutting across the massive formation of friendly tanks with their gun tubes pointing directly towards us. I was horrified, and I could not comprehend how lucky I was to be alive. We radioed the commander and linked up with the company.

A call came over the radio that the Marines had been gassed and we were going to Baghdad. The Marines were fighting in Kuwait, and we were in Iraq. I knew in my heart that we did not have enough troops to fight in Baghdad alone, and I was terrified.

We met little resistance in the minefield, and we were all astonished. Most of the Iraqi soldiers were waving white flags and surrendering. They were terrified, tired, and hungry.

We threw boxes of ready-to-eat meals and water off our tanks as we passed by, for them to eat and drink. It was the kindest act of humanity that I have ever seen. At that time, we were all human beings.

Unfortunately, the rest of the ground war would not be as friendly. After we breached the minefield and entered Iraq, there were dead Iraqi soldiers being eaten by dogs. We dismounted our tanks and stared at the soldiers' corpses. All I thought about was their families. There I was, 19 and getting a first-hand look at war and death.

It was real, and this was war. None of us understood it, whether we were 19 or 40. Nobody said a word.

My mind and body were numb. War is something a person will never completely understand unless they experience it for themselves. My mind went from almost being killed to looking at dead bodies being eaten by dogs.

I was once again focusing on the next mission. I did not have time to think about what I had seen and done. At nightfall, we stopped in a strange place in Iraq that had a lot of curves.

There are not any landmarks in the desert, and we were in "no man's land." Anything could have happened there. It was almost like a maze. It was pitch black.

A Vietnam Veteran said over the radio that this was a good place for an ambush. I wondered how I was supposed to sleep. I laid next to my M-240 machine gun with my 9mm pistol and went to sleep. A tanker knows everything that is going on around him when he is sleep.

Our next mission was to stop the Republican Guard from escaping. Everyone knew that they were the elite, and once again the length of a tank battle loomed in our minds. It was as if we were facing certain death—not because they were better, but because there is so much firepower on the battlefield and tanks lead the way. There is nowhere to hide in the desert, and a tank is completely vulnerable to air strikes.

We moved out in the morning and drove all day. My head kept hitting the top of the tank because I was exhausted. My body literally shut down. We drove all day and fought the Republican Guard that night. It was burning vehicles everywhere.

It was like going towards the World Trade towers when they were falling, instead of fleeing. The driver of the tank was so tired, we almost collided with a burning vehicle. Shots were ringing out everywhere. Tracer rounds and explosions filled the sky. Occasionally, artillery would light up the sky with illumination rounds, so that we could see the entire battlefield.

Heavy machine gun fire filled the night air. It was a complete annihilation of the Republican Guard. We proved to the world that we were unstoppable.

The Dreadnaught battalion kept the history of the 1st Infantry Division intact. All the hard work and training paid off. When the cease-fire was announced, they celebrated because the war was over. The elation on the soldiers' faces was priceless.

You never know how much you love your family until you stare death in the face. It was as if our families were right there with us. I have never seen grown men so happy. They could not have been happier.

However, I was not as happy. My mind was numb, and I had been through hell. Some things happened to me prior to the ground war that made me bitter.

I have never talked about it to this day, and I won't now. That is just the way it is. I sucked it up, and I did my job. Soldiers learn to drive on.

The orders came down for us to provide security for the generals to end the war. I was standing on the ground, talking to one of my friends, and we heard a loud explosion. I immediately ran to my tank, assuming that war had broken out again, but it was engineers destroying enemy weapons.

Some soldiers questioned the decision to end the war so soon. They hoped that they would not return. I knew I was getting out of the Army in November, so it did not matter to me.

We drove through the burning oil fields on the way back to Saudi Arabia. Black smoke and flames were all that we could see. It looked like hell.

At noon, it was pitch black. I touched the tip of my nose and smut was all over my finger. I knew that could not be healthy, and I wondered how it would affect me later.

Now that the war was over, the big question was when are we going home. I was selected to make sure the tanks returned to Saudi Arabia. The truck that carried my tank kept breaking down.

I was forced to wait for a new truck in a location that I was not familiar with. In other words, I was lost. However, I went into the city and met a young Arab boy in a store. He was about 12 or 13 years old.

I called home and my uncle, who is a Vietnam Veteran, answered the phone. I told him that I did not know where I was and I asked him how things were at home. He was calm and told me things were fine. Little did I know that my mother's closest sister was dying of cancer. My mother told me before the war that things would be different when I returned.

Arab women came into the store to look at me. They were dressed in black and wore veils. Their bodies were covered, except for their eyes.

My Arab friend told me they came to flirt with me. They were not supposed to look me in the eyes, but some did anyway. It was not often they were able to see an American soldier in person, and I jumped at the chance to see their culture. Some Afghanistan soldiers came in with long beards and AK-47s. All I had was my 9-millimeter pistol.

They were frowning at me, but I was friendly towards them. I was 19 and fearless. I did not have any idea what kind of situation I was in. I would do anything to find life outside of war.

Furthermore, my Arab friend invited me to his house. I was not supposed to be in that city in the first place, and here I am going to someone's house. I was hesitant, but I went. He had some friends there that spoke English fluently. They were mesmerized by me, and he had a deep love for American soldiers.

He asked me questions like how violent was America and would I ever come back to visit. We sat in a circle, talking and learning about each other's culture. They loved President Bush because he freed them from Saddam Hussein.

When it was time for me to leave, my friend was very sad. It was almost as if he was losing a family member. It made me feel good, and I was proud to be an American soldier. I went back to my tank and moved out again. We came across an Arab man that was very friendly. He asked us if we had any guns, in case Saddam Hussein came back.

We told him, no, but we talked, and he gave us gifts. We met a Bedouin in the desert, and he invited us to dinner. Neither he nor his family spoke English, but we ate and communicated the best we could. It was a wonderful experience. It was another reminder that we were all humans and we should act accordingly.

After about two weeks, I finally made it to Khobar Towers in Saudi Arabia where the rest of my company was. They were glad to see me, and they were worried about me. They did not have any idea where I was, and they had not heard from me. A Vietnam Veteran was anxious to see what I looked like.

I was glad to be with my friends. It was the last stop before we went home. I was finally about to go home. We could go to the mall and around town. However, during public executions, we could not go into the city.

Chapter 6

Impact of War

About two weeks passed, and we left Saudi Arabia. We arrived in Maine to welcome banners and American beer. It was an awesome feeling, but I still was not home yet.

Life after war is devastating and unpredictable. It is far worse than combat itself. I left Desert Storm a changed man, and everyone knew it but me. I was used to living with death, and it had made me numb. I could not walk down the street at night without thinking someone was trying to kill me.

When I was discharged from the Army at the age of 20, I did not know what I wanted to do with my life. All my emotional energy was spent. Alcohol was the only way for me to cope with all the pain I felt inside. People feel like Desert Storm was a war that America won with few casualties. Unfortunately, there are thousands of American soldiers that are sick or already dead.

Oil well fires, pb pills, shots, sand, insects, and chemicals are some causes for these sicknesses. It could be a combination of all of the above. We could have been exposed to low levels of chemicals that were destroyed during and after the war. One theory is that the wind blew low levels of chemicals on us from bombing raids, and from when the engineers destroyed chemical weapons after the war. One thing is for sure, soldiers are complaining about symptoms ranging from chronic fatigue to muscle pain.

After the war, I was running with the battalion flag during physical training, and I ran out of breath. One day I was playing a game of basketball with my cousins, I was breathing extremely hard, and I was out of breath. I was 21 at the time, and I knew that something was wrong, but I was in denial.

Every summer I tried to build wind by jogging, but I just could not do it. I found out that other Desert Storm Veterans are having the same problems. Needless to say, I keep trying no matter how painful or depressing it is.

No one understood. Some of the medication that we used had not been tested. I couldn't walk up a flight of steps without sweating and breathing hard. If I did something as simple as spending time with my family all day, I would be exhausted that night and the next day. I couldn't bend down to tie my shoes because of back pain.

My entire body ached at times, especially when I was working out. If I took medication for some of the symptoms, it felt like someone was beating me in the head with a baseball bat. This is Gulf War Syndrome.

No one wants to be sick. I named just a few symptoms, but there are many more. We are expected to live normal, productive lives when we re-enter society. No one told us about post-traumatic stress disorder (PTSD) unless you had already done something bad.

I did not know that it was normal not to want to be around people after I came back from combat. I went from walking away from fights as a teenager to wanting to kill someone. Everything I tried to do failed, and I had to live with that.

There were mornings when I could not get up to go to work because I was too tired. Alcohol made the fatigue worse. My first job after the war was as an aircraft refueler for a private company. I refueled private and commercial airplanes.

One day I worked a double shift, and by the end of the day, I was making errors like forgetting to put the fuel caps on airplanes. My supervisor told me not to work a double shift anymore. I had no idea at the time that it was because something was wrong with me because I was in denial.

I had to move in with my parents to get back on my feet. Everyone in my family was educated, except me. All three of my sisters had graduated from college and were living on their own. No one understood how I could lay around the house for days and not do anything. Before I was 16, I worked in tobacco fields and bought my own school clothes, even though my parents could have bought them.

I rode my bicycle over 15 miles and over long bridges with my cousins to the blueberry field to pick blueberries. It did not pay a lot of money, but I was young, and I wanted my own money. I played soccer, football, baseball, basketball, and the saxophone.

I had plenty of friends, and I loved to be around people. I was one of the most outgoing guys you could find. Suddenly, the war is over, and I am laying around the house, not looking for a job, and I did not want to be around anyone.

Furthermore, things got worse when I was convicted of two driving while impaired charges. I lost my driver's license for four years. I was losing everything that I had worked for in a short amount of time.

My life had taken a drastic turn for the worst. People were talking about me being different, but I did not care. I found out quickly who my true friends were. I did not have any control of my life, and all I could think about was war.

When I was around my family and friends, I could not sit down and talk to them, nor could I look them in the eyes. I was always on edge, and waiting for something to happen. I was ashamed at the way my life was turning out.

It is hard for me to explain what combat does to the human spirit; you either kill or be killed. In between the actual combat, there are a million ways to be injured or killed. I did the very best I could to live a normal productive life, but nothing worked.

I did not want to drink, but I could not stop. My family was embarrassed at my behavior. I quit going to family reunions, and I did not even go to my mother's retirement party. No one understood the pain I felt inside.

Now that I am older, I understand why people did not understand. Combat becomes a part of who you are. It is not something you can just put behind you, and you get on with your life. If people really understood combat, they would not think about disrespecting a veteran.

All of the veterans that I talked to knew that the D.C. sniper was a veteran. I know veterans whose lives have been turned upside down. They would do anything for a normal life. It is a heavy price to pay to be a warrior. Every step you take on the battlefield could be your last.

After years of moving in and out of my parents' house, I was finally starting to give up. People often asked me if I was back home again, but I remained positive because I knew I would leave again. This time was different; I did not see a way out, and I was tired of getting the same results.

I had an older cousin with a house out in the country; it was the only place on earth that I went to where I did not have to worry about anything. My cousin and his brother accepted me for me. I could drink as much as I wanted and I was at total peace. It was so peaceful that I would drive three hours to go there at any time.

Suddenly, one of the guys in the neighborhood started coming around. I did not go anywhere else in that neighborhood because I was drinking and I did not want any trouble. Sometimes when I would be talking, I noticed this one guy would be looking at me like he hated my guts. I knew the guy did not like me, so I never said anything to him that would set him off.

He must have mistaken me for being weak. I told my friends that this guy was continuing to give me problems and that I did not want to hurt him. This guy was over 6 feet tall. Keep in mind that I was frustrated at the way my life had turned out.

I was at the point where I did not have anything to lose. Finally, one night I was drunk, and some words were said. This time I defended myself. He told me if I said anything else, he was going to drag me all through the yard. I said to myself, you might drag me through this yard, but it will not be tonight.

I immediately started thinking about the war and being killed. I went into the house looking for something to defend myself with, but my cousins talked me out of it. I kept thinking about what he told me, and I hit him in the head with a bottle. My cousins that were there lied and said I hit him for no reason. I had to walk around town with people looking at me like I was crazy.

It was terrible, but it happened. I do not know what would have happened to me if he had not dropped the charges. I ended up getting another DWI the night before I had to go to court. I thought about taking the police officer's gun and running out of the station. Instead, I went home, and my mother had already known about the situation.

Later, my dad had me arrested for taking his car without permission. It was the same officer that arrested me for DWI. He asked me did I remember him, but I was too drunk to recognize him. The guy that I assaulted did not press charges against me, and neither did my dad. My family made me go to a substance abuse center for veterans, and it was the best thing that could have happened to me.

Chapter 7

Rehabilitation

I dreaded the fact that I had to get help. To me, it was a sign of weakness. I was at my lowest point. Things could not have been any worse for me at that time.

My life was down the tubes. My mother and my Aunt Kathy drove me to the veteran's hospital in Salisbury, North Carolina. We spent the night in a cozy hotel because Salisbury is about five hours from New Bern.

The next morning, we drove to the hospital where I would be spending the next 30 days. The admissions officer was a veteran that did two tours in Vietnam. The veteran that was being admitted before me stated that he had hepatitis a and b. I was shocked because you could not tell anything was wrong with him. I said goodbye to my family, not knowing that my life would change forever.

The first thing that I noticed was that the veterans took a lot of pills. The first thing I did was see the doctor, and I left his office with a brown bag full of medicine. I could not believe it because I was still in denial. I was walking down the hall with my pills, wondering what was happening to me.

Everyone, including the staff, was staring at me because I was so young. I was 28 at the time. One of the nurses walked up to me in the cafeteria and asked me how old I was. They all knew if I was there then something was terribly wrong.

The first two days were rough. I felt like I made the wrong decision. However, I started making friends, and my outlook changed. One of my friends was a truck driver with a cocaine problem. He killed some people in an accident, and he had trouble sleeping at night. His attitude was terrible, and people did not like being around him.

He told me that since I was there, the only places left for me to go were prison or the graveyard. He told me if I was there, my life was over and I was in big trouble. Then he told me to look at the sign outside; the sign said, "Mental Ward, 4th Floor." I knew if I kept doing what I was doing, that was my next stop.

I was at the breaking point of my life. I made up my mind then that I would never drink again. The truck driver was not a Vietnam Veteran, but he was in the Army during that time. That was his 15th trip to rehab. He opened my eyes up to the road I was on, and I really appreciate him for that.

However, I learned how to play chess while I was in jail and it gave me something to do. Chess gave me a chance to learn how to live without drinking. My cousin Boo, who is like the brother I never had, inspired me to learn the game. It also gave me the opportunity to break away from my friend because his attitude was so bad.

I have always had a tremendous amount of respect for Vietnam Veterans. I had never heard any war stories from one, but that would soon change. My Uncle Wink is a Vietnam Veteran, and I have always admired how he kept his life together. A guy named Walter moved into my four-man room, and he was a Vietnam Veteran.

The next day in group therapy, the counselor asked him why he was there. He told her it might be to help someone else. Walt was an airborne sniper in Vietnam, and he had been to several treatment centers. One of the first questions I asked was, "When does the nightmare end?" The Vietnam Veterans told me it does not end.

These were not counselors that learned from books. These were the men that fought and saw their buddies killed, and lived to talk about it. For nine years, I was all alone. No one understood how I felt—not even my mother, and she understands everything. It was all coming together now.

I found a new family in Salisbury. I found out why I felt like that, and it was normal. I had been around all types of people in my life, but these men were different. They had problems on top of problems. Add alcohol and drugs to PTSD, and you have some real problems.

One veteran told me he took 14 pills every day. Another said he was tired of it all and thought about committing suicide. Late one evening, the guy with hepatitis played and sang the most beautiful song I have ever heard on his guitar, about being homeless and Jesus.

Just because we were there did not mean that Jesus did not love us, too. We all had major problems, and we were looking for help. I was closer to God there than I had ever been in my life.

During the day, we went to classes on learning how to stay clean and sober to learning what stress and drugs do to the body. One night, the Vietnam Veterans discussed the war in my room. It was very intense.

They were sharing poems that they wrote during the war. The poems revealed how afraid they were and how badly they wanted to go home. Later that night, one of the veterans kept pacing back and forth through the room. I tried to calm him down.

I understood why they do not talk about the details of the war. Walt told me I was sleep-walking one night and he told me everything I did. I remembered doing some things like going to the bathroom, but I did not remember everything. When we were getting ready for bed that night, he opened the curtains so he could see everything.

I asked him to tell me some stories about the war, and he did. He said he was ordered to go down and inspect a tunnel and found three dead American soldiers with their penises cut off and stuck in their mouths. One of the guys was talking about "Puff the Magic Dragon" saving him in one of his poems. One of the lines went something like, "Puff the Magic Dragon, please get us out of here." The sadness and seriousness of the tone of his voice were shocking.

It was all starting to come together. Some questions I had were finally being answered. Group therapy was held once a day. The counselors focused on one person daily and helped him to solve his problems.

That is when I realized how wrong a person can be when judging someone you do not know. Several people in my group had cancer, and I did not know it. It was easy for me to listen to their problems and come up with my own solutions.

However, when it was my turn, it was not as easy as I thought it would be. My counselor started asking me questions that I did not like, and I became extremely angry. I got out of my seat and started walking around.

The next day at group therapy, nobody wanted to sit beside me. From that point on, the people in my group had more respect for me. The more time I spent there, the more I started thinking about the direction that my life was going in.

It was becoming clearer that I was not alone in my struggle. I learned to stay away from parties and my old friends. Anything that could cause me to relapse was considered a trigger, and I had to stay away at all costs. I learned valuable lessons there that I still apply today.

Chapter 8

Life After Rehabilitation

Now that I was back home, I had to learn how to live sober again. It was like starting from scratch. Changing my friends was the hardest part of the process. I was used to living on the edge my entire adult life.

Luckily, one of my best friends was changing his life also, and we made the transition together. I realized that I had to find something to take the place of drinking, so I played chess as much as I could. However, everything was different.

My mind was changing drastically, and I was starting to see things clearer. At the same time, I did not have any means of coping with the war. In that respect, I was alone again. I was fighting two major battles: addiction and combat. I began searching for answers to my problems because that was the only chance I had to live a productive life.

The price you pay for being a warrior is high. Often people commit suicide or homicide after returning from war. Others live a life of drugs and alcohol. I hope this book will put combat in its proper perspective.

Operation Iraqi Freedom put me right back in Desert Storm. It was almost unbearable. I could not believe it. I knew that the only reason the war had not started earlier was because the equipment was not in place yet. It takes months to get the equipment in position for battle.

I used to joke about watching the next war on television. When the deadline passed for Saddam Hussein to leave Iraq, I watched the news waiting for the intense air raid. Instead, it was extremely calm. I told my friend that the war had probably already started.

The United States knows how to use the element of surprise. Our battle plan was great in Desert Storm, so I thought it would be used again. The air raid did not weaken the spirits of the enemy.

In Desert Storm, we used B-52 bombers escorted by fighters to devastate our opponent. The Iraqi prisoners of war would lay face-down when an aircraft passed by. The power was turned off immediately, and we hit every target that enabled them to wage war.

However, the ground war started too fast. There were not enough ground forces to fight that kind of war. I was devastated when I found out that the ground war had started because I knew there were not enough troops.

I felt like I was right there with them fighting. My mind and my spirit were with them. Then I realized that the reason the ground war started so soon was because they had to secure the oil fields.

The plan was to have more ground troops to invade through Turkey, but Turkey would not agree. The ground troops fought a tremendous fight. All I could think about was how lucky I was to be alive. I realized why it was so hard for me to get past the war, and why I had changed so much. I had nothing to be ashamed of.

I understand now why my family did not understand the way I felt. You have to experience it for yourself, to get the proper understanding. I did my job to the best of my ability, and I put my life on the line. It changed my outlook on life, and I made some terrible decisions. I learned not to take anything for granted and swore to live my life to the fullest for as long as I could.

America is a wonderful place to live. You can be anything you choose to be here. This kind of freedom is not cheap. It comes with a heavy price that a warrior pays. I wish I would have known what to expect after the war was over.

I hope this book will help someone understand what a warrior experiences after war. I did not have a clue that what I was going through was normal for combat veterans. My parents stood by me, even though my life was a living hell. My mother accepted and encouraged me, despite my situation. My dad supported me and got me the help that I needed.

Chapter 9

Problems Aren't Coincidental

Thereafter, I learned that problems in life aren't a coincidence. Problems are sent by God. The Bible refers to problems as temptations, tests, and fiery trials. Bishop T.D. Jakes said that "no one can escape the courtroom of God; your faith must stand trial." What happened to me was ordered by God, and He gave me the power to overcome it.

Beloved, think it not strange concerning the fiery trial which is to try you, as though some strange thing happened unto you: But rejoice, inasmuch as ye are partakers of Christ's sufferings; that, when his glory shall be revealed, ye may be glad also with exceeding joy. 1 Peter 4:12-13 (KJV)

Wherein ye greatly rejoice, though now for a season, if need be, ye are in heaviness through manifold temptations: That the trial of your faith, being much more precious than of gold that perisheth, though it be tried with fire, might be found unto praise and honour and glory at the appearing of Jesus Christ: 1 Peter 1:6-7 (KJV)

The trial of our faith is more precious than gold to God. Faith, family, finances, health, and relationships will stand trial in life. No one is exempt.

There hath no temptation taken you but such as is common to man: but God is faithful, who will not suffer you to be tempted above that ye are able; but will with the temptation also make a way to escape, that ye may be able to bear it. 1 Corinthians 10:13 (KJV)

It's always someone who's been through what you're going through. God won't put more on you than you can handle. He's made a way out of the problem that He gave you, but it's up to you to take it.

What happened to me wasn't a coincidence. I fought using the Abrams tank in the Gulf War, and now I use the Abrahamic Covenant on the battlefield of life. God used Dr. Jay Snell to teach me the covenant, and my nickname is Jay.

Chapter 10

How to Overcome

I learned about the Everlasting Covenant while attending North Carolina Agricultural and Technical State University from 2001-2005. The Everlasting Covenant is God's promise to bless man if we obey His commandments. It's also known as the Abrahamic Covenant. You will overcome life's greatest challenges by using the Abrahamic Covenant. It guarantees success in every area of life beginning with salvation.

And the angel of the Lord called unto Abraham out of heaven the second time, And said, By myself have I sworn, saith the Lord, for because thou hast done this thing, and hast not withheld thy son, thine only son:

That in blessing I will bless thee, and in multiplying I will multiply thy seed as the stars of the heaven, and as the sand which is upon the sea shore; and thy seed shall possess the gate of his enemies; And in thy seed shall all the nations of the earth be blessed; because thou hast obeyed my voice. Genesis 22:15-18 (KJV)

This sounded too good to be true when I read it for the 1st time. I couldn't believe that Almighty God swore to bless me! This is the scripture that revolutionized my thinking and my life. I knew that I had found what I was looking for, and I started doing research on it. Think long and hard about this covenant, God Himself swore to bless you!

The word of God is the most powerful force on Earth. The Abrahamic Covenant is what I used to graduate from college in 2005. It solves all my problems. It's God's unbeatable weapon on the battlefield of life. I'll go deeper into the covenant in my next book, but this is how it works.

First and foremost, it doesn't get any better than partaking in a loving relationship with God. Many people are unhappy because they put money, people, and material things over God. Look at how many rich people, celebrities, and athletes end up in bad situations.

And I will establish my covenant between me and thee and thy seed after thee in their generations for an everlasting covenant, to be a God unto thee, and to thy seed after thee. Genesis 17:7 (KJV)

And if ye be Christ's, then are ye Abraham's seed, and heirs according to the promise. Galatians 3:29 (KJV)

The seed of Abraham are Christians from every nation. God blessed Abraham because he obeyed Him. We're not going to obey every commandment from God because we're not perfect. We strive to obey every commandment, but when we fall short, the blood of Jesus washes away our sins. How great is God?

A covenant is an agreement. The Greek word for testament is covenant. God made the promise to Abraham, and his seed. God told Abraham to circumcise himself and his seed as a sign of the covenant.

The blood of lambs was used as the substitute for God's blood until He shed His own blood. Jesus was God in the flesh, and the blood that Jesus shed was the blood of Almighty God. God came to earth in the form of Jesus to complete the covenant. Man shed blood by circumcision, and God Himself shed blood by being beaten and crucified.

This is my covenant, which ye shall keep, between me and you and thy seed after thee; Every man child among you shall be circumcised. And ye shall circumcise the flesh of your foreskin; and it shall be a token of the covenant betwixt me and you. Genesis 17:10-11(KJV)

Take heed therefore unto yourselves, and to all the flock, over the which the Holy Ghost hath made you overseers, to feed the church of God, which he hath purchased with his own blood. Acts 20:28 (KJV)

Now the God of peace, that brought again from the dead our Lord Jesus, that great shepherd of the sheep, through the blood of the everlasting covenant, Hebrews 13:20 (KJV)

And Abraham was old, and well stricken in age: and the Lord had blessed Abraham in all things. Genesis 24:1 (KJV)

I knew that I would graduate from college when I found out about the covenant. I knew that If I was obedient to God, He had to bless me. I had a promise from God that was backed by His sworn oath, and sealed in His own blood! The blood of Jesus washed away my sins, so my past was irrelevant. All I had to do was put what I learned in the Bible into action.

God blessed Abraham in all things. Abraham's grandson Jacob wrestled God all night, refusing to let go until God blessed him! (See Gen. 32:24-30) I was used to fighting with the odds against me. However, the odds were against me in the natural realm, but I had a tremendous advantage in the spirit realm. **Refusing to quit using the word of God is the key**

to overcoming life's greatest challenges! Do what the bible says and believe.

My greatest challenge in college was a course that I didn't understand, and it was 2 parts to it. I was totally lost after the 1st couple of classes. I acquired a tutor, but that didn't help. I would get headaches when I tried to study for the class. I started thinking hard about the covenant, and the weapons that I had to use to win this battle.

Quitting wasn't an option, and I kept going to class hoping that the professor wouldn't call on me to answer a question. However, I knew that I had to become more aggressive in the spirit realm, so I volunteered to clean my church. It was one of the best feelings that I've ever had, I was obedient, and I knew God had to keep His promise.

The only thing that I knew on the final exam was my name, and I still had to take part 2 of the course to graduate! I was banking totally on the Abrahamic Covenant, and I graduated. God handled part 2 for me Himself. I do what the scripture tells me to do, and I believe God will do what the scripture says He will do. Life is an open book test.

For the weapons of our warfare are not carnal, but mighty through God to the pulling down of strong holds;) Casting down imaginations, and every high thing that exalteth itself against the knowledge of God, and bringing into captivity every thought to the obedience of Christ; 2 Corinthians 10:4-5 (KJV)

Think about the scriptures, and how God swore to bless you instead of thinking about your problem. The Devil made me think about every terrible thing that I had ever done, but I used God's weapons to defeat him. Commit thy works unto the Lord, and thy thoughts shall be established. Proverbs 16:3 (KJV)

Then Peter opened his mouth, and said, Of a truth I perceive that God is no respecter of persons: Acts 10:34 (KJV)

We're all the same in God's eyes. He promised, and swore to bless us because He creates problems for us that will make us doubt. Is any thing too hard for the Lord? Genesis 18:14 (KJV)

If ye abide in me, and my words abide in you, ye shall ask what ye will, and it shall be done unto you. John 15:7 (KJV) I wrote this scripture on an index card and carried it in my pocket during my toughest semester in college. When the grades came out, God was right there just like He said He would be. Nothing is more powerful than the word of God. It will change your circumstances, and it's the key to life!

Think about How awesome God is, and what He promised you. God is talking to you through the bible. God loves us!

Love worketh no ill to his neighbour: therefore love is the fulfilling of the law. Romans 13:10 (KJV) Love alone wins the war. Hate comes from the Devil, it doesn't matter who's teaching it or doing it.

But the fruit of the Spirit is love, joy, peace, longsuffering, gentleness, goodness, faith, Meekness, temperance: against such there is no law. Galatians 5:22-23 (KJV) This is how you know who God's people are! Wherefore by their fruits ye shall know them. Matthew 7:20 (KJV)

Two of my favorite weapons in spiritual warfare are fasting and honoring the Sabbath Day. They worked wonders for me in college. Don't stop using your weapons (scriptures) until you win, this is the key! This principle is taught throughout the bible, you can use any scripture. You must be relentless with the word of God, and never quit.

But as for me, when they were sick, my clothing was sackcloth: I humbled my soul with fasting; and my prayer returned into mine own bosom. Psalms 35:13 (KJV)

And when he was come into the house, his disciples asked him privately, Why could not we cast him out? And he said unto them, This kind can come forth by nothing, but by prayer and fasting. Mark 9:28-29 (KJV)

For whatsoever things were written aforetime were written for our learning, that we through patience and comfort of the scriptures might have hope. Romans 15:4 (KJV) It doesn't matter what you're facing, use these weapons relentlessly and you'll win. Obedience will activate the Abrahamic Covenant.

If thou turn away thy foot from the sabbath, from doing thy pleasure on my holy day; and call the sabbath a delight, the holy of the Lord, honourable; and shalt honour him, not doing thine own ways, nor finding thine own pleasure, nor speaking thine own words:

Then shalt thou delight thyself in the Lord; and I will cause thee to ride upon the high places of the earth, and feed thee with the heritage of Jacob thy father: for the mouth of the Lord hath spoken it. Isaiah 58:13-14 (KJV)

Some people think that the covenant is void because it's in the Old Testament. That's false because it's everlasting. Circumcision of the flesh is void because Jesus completed the covenant. In fact, here is the Abrahamic Covenant in the New Testament.

For God is not unrighteous to forget your work and labour of love, which ye have shewed toward his name, in that ye have ministered to the saints, and do minister. And we desire that every one of you do shew the same diligence to the full assurance of hope unto the end: That ye be not slothful, but followers of them who through faith and patience inherit the promises. Hebrews 6:10-12 (KJV)

For when God made promise to Abraham, because he could swear by no greater, he sware by himself, Saying, Surely blessing I will bless thee, and multiplying I will multiply thee. And so, after he had patiently endured, he obtained the promise. For men verily swear by the greater: and an oath for confirmation is to them an end of all strife. Hebrews 6:13-16 (KJV)

Wherein God, willing more abundantly to shew unto the heirs of promise the immutability of his counsel, confirmed it by an oath: That by two immutable things, in which it was impossible for God to lie, we might have a strong consolation, who have fled for refuge to lay hold upon the hope set before us: Which hope we have as an anchor of the soul, both sure and stedfast, and which entereth into that within the veil; Hebrews 6:17-19 (KJV)

God's sworn oath to us ends all doubt! I'll overcome every problem that I'll ever face in life because God's promise is sure, steadfast, and it anchors my soul! It's my refuge during the storms of life. Faith and patience is how we inherit our promises. If you're sick, God swore to heal you.

He promised to bless your finances too, He covered everything, it's unchangeable. I handle every problem in life by using the Abrahamic Covenant. God promised to bless me in all things just like He promised Abraham!

You won't get this kind of teaching everywhere because it's God's secret, and now He's sharing it with you. The covenant is a secret. The secret of the Lord is with them that fear him; and he will shew them his covenant. Psalms 25:14 (KJV)

It doesn't matter what your problem is, you'll win if you use this covenant. Share this book with friends, family, and Veterans. One word from God can change your life.

Recommended Reading

Snell, Jay. How to Be Healed Using Spiritual Warfare (Jay Snell Evangelistic Association, 1997).

Snell, Jay. How To Obtain Abraham's Blessings Volume Four (Jay Snell Evangelistic Association, 1993).

Snell, Jay. How To Amass Abrahamic Wealth (Jay Snell Evangelistic Association, 1995).

About the Author

Joseph fought in the Gulf War as an M-1 Tanker in the legendary 1st Infantry Division, also known as the Big Red One. His mission was to lead the attack on the enemy mine field while being attacked with chemical and biological weapons. It was a suicide mission, and he was awarded the Valorous Unit Award for extraordinary heroism in war. He graduated from North Carolina Agricultural and Technical State University in 2005 with a Bachelor of Social Work Degree. The chair of the Department of Sociology and Social Work, Dr. Sarah V. Kirk, inspired him to write a book about the war and his experiences. Joseph has a passion for reading, writing, football, and golf.

Contact Joseph

Website: neversurrenderthebook.com

Email: joe@neversurrenderthebook.com

Twitter: twitter.com/authorjosephgeo

Made in the USA
Monee, IL
05 February 2021